UNPLANTED
YET
Flourishing

A Poetic Journey Through Infertility, Loss & Healing

By Melba

Unplanted, Yet Flourishing: A Poetic Journey Through Infertility, Loss & Healing

© 2025 by Melba

poetic.nectar.collective@gmail.com

ISBN: 979-8-9985739-0-3

Published by: Melba

Cover Design & Interior Layout: Melba

Illustrations: Melba

This book is a work of creative nonfiction and poetry. The experiences expressed within are personal and may not reflect every reader's journey. If you are struggling, please seek support from a trusted professional or community.

Printed in the United States of America

Author's Note

My name is Melba, and this book is a piece of my story.

For many years, my husband and I tried to grow our family. We went through loss after loss. Surgeries. Treatments. We hoped. We grieved. We waited. And through it all, I felt invisible—like no one really talked about what this journey feels like.

Writing became my way through it. I didn't write these poems as a project. I wrote them because I needed somewhere to put the pain. Somewhere to feel seen. Somewhere to start healing.

That healing didn't come all at once, but it came. And over time, I created a life I love—one that's soft, full, and mine.

My husband and I moved to a quiet place by the sea —just us— surrounded by nature, light, and the kind of stillness we had been craving. Here, our days are shaped by the outdoors, by ease, and by the quiet joy of simply being together.

My life may not look the way I once imagined it, but it's beautiful in its own way—and it's enough.

If you've ever felt unseen, I hope these words meet you gently. Thank you for holding them.

—Melba

Before the Bloom

Come as you are.

This book was written from the quiet—
the moments between grief and healing,
between what was hoped for and what never came.
It won't offer you answers or steps to follow.
But it will offer presence.
A place to land.
A companion when the ache is too quiet to explain.

You don't have to believe in anything to belong here.
You don't need to be ready to heal.
You don't need to let go.

These pages are here to sit with you in the ache.
To say what often goes unsaid.
To soften the silence around invisible loss.
To remind you—
you were never meant to carry it alone.

Let this be your garden,
your stillness,
your mirror,
your breath.

There is space here for all of you.

Table of Contents

Journey 1: The Weight of Silence............................1

Journey 2: The Body's Story...........................…17

Journey 3: Love, Loss & Rebuilding................…..........35

Journey 4: Breaking the Silence..............................49

Journey 5: Redefining Self, Redefining Motherhood....…...59

Journey 6: Healing & Enoughness...........................71

Journey 7: Light After the Storm..................….........87

Poetic Nectar Collective: A Sanctuary of Words.....……...99

Guide to Healing: A Soft Offering.................…..........107

Final Reflection...............….................................115

Appendix: Where to Find Light (Resources & Support)....117

Discussion Questions & Reflection...........................121

Acknowledgments...123

JOURNEY ONE

The Weight of Silence

Silence is more than the absence of words.

It is the weight of unasked questions,
the quiet suffocation of expectations,
the invisible grief we are told to carry alone.

This journey holds the sting of labels we never claimed, the quiet solidarity of women who wear their pain like a shared secret.

But this is also where we begin to break free.

Because our bodies are not puzzles to be solved.
Because our worth was never in their hands to name.
Because we are more than their silence.

This is where we begin to reclaim ourselves.

"When Will You?" – The Blade of Expectation

"When are you having kids?"

The question hangs in the air like a blade, sharp and careless, cutting through the quiet.

I smile, a reflex polished by years of practice,
and tuck the truth behind my teeth —
a flame too hot to speak, too bright to swallow.

They don't see the storm inside me,
the way my heart cracks under the weight of their
curiosity, their expectations, their need to name what
I cannot give.

My womb is not a calendar,
not a clock ticking toward their dreams.
It is a horizon, open and endless,
a place where I define the sunrise,
a space where my worth is not a question.

Prescriptions for a Broken Dream

"Try yoga, try kale, try God."

Their advice pours over me like acid rain,
each drop a reminder of what I've already tried.

I've swallowed mountains of hope,
spent my savings on promises,
let doctors map my insides like uncharted territory.

And still, my body remains a locked door,
a mystery even I can't solve.

No one asks if I want the key.

No one asks if I am tired of the endless cycle
of hope and heartbreak.

They just keep offering solutions,
as if my pain is a problem they can fix.

But my body is not a puzzle.
And I am not a problem to be solved.

A Name Unspoken

I never got to say your name.
I never got to whisper it into the night,
to trace it into the sky with my fingertips.

But I felt you.

For a moment, I was a home,
a heartbeat wrapped around a smaller one.

And then—
you were gone.

They do not call me a mother.

There is no birth certificate,
no tiny footprints pressed into ink.

But I know you were here.
And I will carry you,
even if the world never says your name.

Drink This, Do That

They said to drink herbs from a root I couldn't
pronounce,
to press oils into my belly at dawn,
to do headstands after sex
and whisper hope into my tea.

And I did.

Because when you are desperate,
even magic seems logical.
Even nonsense feels like medicine.

I wanted it to work.

I wanted anything to work.

I wanted to believe
that effort meant outcome,
that devotion could rewrite biology,
that maybe—just maybe—
hope was stronger than science.

But some prayers
never make it past the skin.

The Language of Silence

We pass each other in grocery aisles,
eyes down, hearts heavy with the same secret.

Our silence is a language only we understand—
a quiet nod, a fleeting glance,
a recognition of the ache we both carry.

We don't speak, but we don't need to.

Our pain is a thread that binds us,
invisible but unbreakable.

One day, we will find the courage
to let our voices rise like a chorus of strength,
to turn our whispers into war cries,
and our silence into song.

The Life That Never Was

There was a heartbeat once—
or at least, I think there was.

There was a moment,
before the silence,
before the doctor's voice
became an echo I couldn't outrun.

There was a dream,
a future I could almost touch.

Tiny hands.
First words.
A name I never got to say.

And then—
there was nothing.

I left the clinic with empty hands,
but my body still felt full of you.

As if grief had taken your place.
As if my womb had learned the shape of loss
and refused to let it go.

They call it miscarriage—
as if I simply misplaced you,
as if I might find you again someday.

But I know better.
I did not lose you.
You were taken.

And I am still learning
how to plant gardens in the space
you left behind.

The Storm Inside

I wear my pain in silence,
not because I have no words,
but because the world is too loud to hear them.

They celebrate life,
while I grieve the absence of it.

Smiling through the ache,
carrying hope like a blade I refuse to lay down.

They don't see the silent storm,
the prayers stitched into my ribs,
the whispered deals with the universe—
"just one chance, just one heartbeat."

But I am still here.

Still breathing.
Still standing in the eye of the storm.

And for now,
that is my rebellion.

Wilderness, Not Wasteland

They tally my worth in ultrasounds,
in empty cribs, in silent nights.

They call me barren,
as if my body is a field that failed to yield.

But I am not a field—
I am an ocean, deep and untamed,
pulling the tides of love and grief,
holding life in unseen ways.

Let them call me barren.
I am a force, not a failure.

Inheritance

The wind doesn't wonder if it should return.
It just does.
Like bees moving between blooms,
like salmon tracing rivers back to where they
began—
everything in nature remembers.

The turtles bury life beneath warm sand,
never waiting to see what hatches.
Even the trees split open with seed
as if letting go is what they were made for.

Creation isn't questioned.
It's woven into the marrow—
a silent command passed down
through cells, wings, roots.

And still, here I am.
With hands that never held
what my body reached for.
With rhythm in my bones,
but no one to carry the song forward.

The ache is ancient.
It isn't just mine.
It belongs to the soil,
to the mothers of mothers of mothers,
to every creature that knew how to make
and wasn't able to.

Still, I rise.
Still, I root.
Still, I create.

Even if it's not what nature expected of me.

The Window

They don't tell you
how narrow it is—
this window of time.
A fleeting breath,
for everything to align:
body, breath, love,
and something unseen.

I watched the moon,
hoping my body would follow.
Held my breath
between morning and maybe.

We tried to make a life
with a clock
ticking beneath the sheets.

And when it passed—
when the window closed—
I sat in the quiet
with my hands still open.

JOURNEY TWO

The Body's Story

A body is not just flesh and bone.
It is a story, a battleground, a home.

It holds memories of what it has carried,
and echoes of what it has lost.

This journey is for the bodies that have been
questioned, measured, misunderstood.

For the ones that have been called broken,
and for the ones learning to love themselves again.

Your body is more than what it can create.
More than what it has endured.
More than what the world has told you it should be.

Your body is yours.

Ultrasound Rooms and Empty Chairs

The walls hum with quiet anticipation,
a sterile silence heavy with waiting.
A monitor flickers to life,
but there is nothing to see.

The doctor clears their throat.
Their voice is gentle, rehearsed.
"Let's try again next time."

I nod, pretending not to feel
the way the air shifts around me,
the way my own breath feels foreign.

I walk out,
past swollen bellies and soft baby cries,
past the smiling faces in waiting rooms
who have not learned how to grieve hope.

In the hallway,
I forget where I parked.
I forget what day it is.
I sit behind the wheel
and stare at nothing
until the world comes back into focus.

There are errands to run.
Emails waiting.

A life that didn't pause
just because I did.

And still—
somehow—
I start the engine.

I am learning to live beyond the waiting.
To stand in this body, just as it is.
Not because it's easy—
but because it's what I have.

Red Again

It always begins with a whisper—
a flutter in my chest,
a calendar check,
a breath held longer than usual.

Maybe.
Could it be?
This time… maybe.

I walk slower.
Eat gently.
Feel every ache
as if it might mean
something new
is growing.

And then—
red.
A bloom
I never asked for
unfolding again.

Hope washes down the drain
with a sigh I don't mean to release.

I wrap myself in quiet.
In soft clothes.
In stillness.

21

There is no announcement,
no breaking news—
just the silence
of a womb
not yet chosen.

The Tests, the Pills, the Needles

They hand me another prescription,
another round of hope in a bottle.
They say,
"Let's adjust your dosage."
"Just give it time."
"Have faith."

But there is no pill
for a heart
that is tired of beating
for something
it may never hold.

This Body is Not a Failure

They call it infertility,
as if my body is a machine that won't start,
as if I am a field that refused to bloom.

They count what my body has not done,
but they do not count the ways it has carried me.

This body breathes and bends.
This body has held hands, built strength, danced in
the rain.
This body has known pleasure, laughter, and long
walks under the sun.

This body is not broken.
This body is not a failure.

These Hips

They told me
my hips were made for babies—
wide like the women before me,
curved like prophecy,
a cradle shaped by generations.

They said,
you're built for it.
As if my body had a duty
etched in bone.
As if softness meant destiny.

But these hips,
they've held more than children—
they've held storms.
Held me upright
when the ground fell out.
Held the weight
of grief I never asked for.

They sway with music still,
move with stories untold,
rooted in ancestors who danced
barefoot in dirt
and carried more than anyone saw.

No child grew here.
But don't you dare say
these hips failed.
They bloomed resilience.
They are altars.
They are mine.

Not Just a Vessel

For so long, I thought my body was only meant
to be a home for someone else.

But my body is mine.

It carries me through morning stretches,
through long walks in the sun,
through the joy of movement and the quiet of rest.

My body is not an apology.
My body is not unfinished work.
My body is worthy, whole, alive.

The Body That Fought Itself

No one told me
that a body could wage war against itself.

That pain could coil itself around my womb,
that I could bleed for weeks,
that cysts and fibroids could grow inside me
like ghosts I never invited.

Doctors dismissed me.
"You are overreacting."
"Some women just have difficult cycles."
"Come back when you want children."

As if my pain was only real
if it threatened the life inside me—
as if I was only worth healing
if I was preparing to bring life into the world.

But my body matters,
even when it is just my own.

Even when it is only fighting for itself.

Mirror, Mirror

I have spent years learning to look at my own reflection
without searching for something missing.

I have measured myself in all the wrong ways—
in pounds, in timelines, in empty spaces.

But today, I see the woman staring back at me,

and she is soft and strong.
She is resilient and radiant.
She is whole, just as she is.

And for the first time,
I do not look away.

Riverbeds

My scars are not cracks—
they are riverbeds
shaped by storm,
carving paths through what tried to bury me.

Each jagged line,
a current of survival—
proof that I moved through it,
and didn't stay broken.

I am not ruined.
I am water—
still flowing,
still returning,
still mine.

This Body Remembers

This body
was once a garden
you prayed over.

Now it holds
the ache of every season
you did not harvest.

Hormones like winds—
unpredictable, sharp.
Scars in places
no one can see.
A tenderness that lingers
even on quiet days.

You learned to live
between blood tests
and breathwork,
to wear softness
like armor.

And still—
despite the ache,
the fire,
the unraveling—
this body stood
beneath every storm.

And did not fall.

The Cost of Hope

They told me to "just keep trying,"
as if hope were free,
as if it didn't come wrapped in invoices,
hidden fees, and whispered "unfortunately"s.

They did not see the spreadsheets,
the savings drained,
the whispered conversations of

"Can we afford another round?"
"Do we try again, or do we let go?"

They did not feel the weight of the choice—
the one that no couple should have to make.

To risk financial ruin for the possibility of life,
or to close the door and carry the ache.

Infertility is not just a struggle of the body.
It is a battle of the bank account,
a debt of hope and heartbreak,
a cost no one prepares you for.

And yet—
we pay.

Because how do you put a price on maybe?

The Body I Am Becoming

This body has known pain
and still, it holds me—
not in spite of,
but because of it.

Every scar,
every tear,
is a testament
to the strength it took
to survive this journey.

I will not apologize
for the body that fought itself,
for the one that still rises—
a force, not a failure.

In the quiet of the night,
when the weight of expectation
tries to erase me,
I remember:

I am still here.

And this body?
It is not broken.
It is becoming.

JOURNEY THREE
Love, Loss & Rebuilding

Love does not stay the same after loss.
It stretches, fractures, reshapes itself.

Some days, love feels like an anchor, steady and
strong.
Other days, it feels like a wound that won't close.

This journey is for the ones who have learned to
love
through the silence, the waiting, the heartbreak.

For the ones who have lost,
but still choose to love anyway.

The Space Between Us

There were mornings
I could feel you
but couldn't reach you.

We sat inches apart—
coffee cooling between us—
and still,
you felt miles away.

Grief made ghosts of us.
Not gone,
but drifting.

I whispered
what I couldn't say out loud:
Come back.
Or let me go.
But don't leave me
somewhere in between.

Two People, One Grief

We stood in the same room
but carried different storms.

You spoke in silence.
I wept through action.
We both ached—
just not in the same rhythm.

You searched for reasons.
I searched for softness.
And somehow,
our grief became
a room with no doors.

Still,
I know you were there.
I know you held pain
even if you held it
differently than I did.

Love Is Not a Cure

Love does not erase grief.

It does not stitch together what has been torn,
or return what was taken.

Love does not undo the ache,
does not rewrite the past,
does not fill the spaces that still ache to be whole.

Love cannot bring back the heartbeat that faded,
cannot rebuild the life that never came to be.

And yet—

Love is what sits with you in the quiet.
It is the hand that does not let go,
the presence that does not turn away.

Love does not fix the brokenness.
But it is the thing that stays, even when nothing else
does.

It does not ask you to move on.
Only to keep moving.

Where the Fire Went

The fire didn't leave you.
It just moved—
settled into the curve of your shoulders,
the quiet of your stomach,
the pause between your breaths.

Every "I'm okay"
was a match struck in your throat,
then swallowed whole.

You became a house that learned
how to hold the heat
without going up in flames.

You stopped burning.
But you never went cold.

That warmth lives in you now—
not as fury,
but as something steadier.

You use it to soften rooms,
to sit beside others in the dark
without needing to speak.

That's where the fire went.
Not gone.
Just changed.

And Then There Was One

We were all in it together once—
timing cycles,
sharing updates,
hoping for double lines.

For a while,
our stories mirrored each other—
uncertain,
repetitive,
softened by understanding.

But slowly,
they began to shift.
One by one,
they got their news,
their nursery plans,
their happy endings.

And I was still waiting.
Still am.

The messages changed.
Fewer check-ins.
More baby pictures.
Less space for what I hadn't received.

I celebrate them.
Truly.
But it's hard to explain
the silence that comes
when you're the only one
left in the waiting room.

Still, I wake each day
and open the blinds,
trusting the light
to reach even me.

The Love That Held Me

He watched me unravel—
piece by piece,
grief slipping through my fingers
like sand too fine to hold.

He did not try to fix me.
He did not tell me to be strong.

Instead, he sat in the wreckage with me,
held my trembling hands,
and whispered,
"Even here, I love you."

And I realized—
love is not in the answers,
but in the quiet places
where nothing needs to be said.

The Kind of Love That Survives

It's not the kind of love
they write about in stories—
not all candlelight and rescue.

It's quiet,
often strained,
held together by glances
when words feel too far away.

It survived
the waiting rooms,
the silences,
the moments we almost gave up.

It cracked,
but didn't collapse.
It bent under the weight
and still chose to stay.

This love didn't save us.
But it stood with us
when nothing else could.

After the Bleeding

He touches me
like I haven't changed.
Like this body is still ours.
Like nothing ever fell
from the garden inside me.

But something did.

And some nights,
when his hands remember spring,
mine remember
what never came to bloom.

I don't know how to ask for space
without wilting him.
I don't know how to be close
without betraying
the ache that hums
like thunder beneath my skin.

So I stay still.
I listen.
I try to be present—
but part of me
is counting moon cycles,
listening for roots
that never took.

There is nothing wrong
with his love.
But I am still learning
how to let warmth in—
slowly,
like sunlight
after rain.

Rebuilding Love

We are not the same
as we were before.

Our love has been broken,
but it is not gone.

We rebuild in small moments—
in the quiet of the night
when our hands brush by accident,
in the soft laughter
that reminds us of who we are,
even when we don't feel whole.

Grief has made space for something new,
something stronger,
not in spite of the loss,
but because of it.

Love is not what it was,
but it is still here.

JOURNEY FOUR

Breaking the Silence

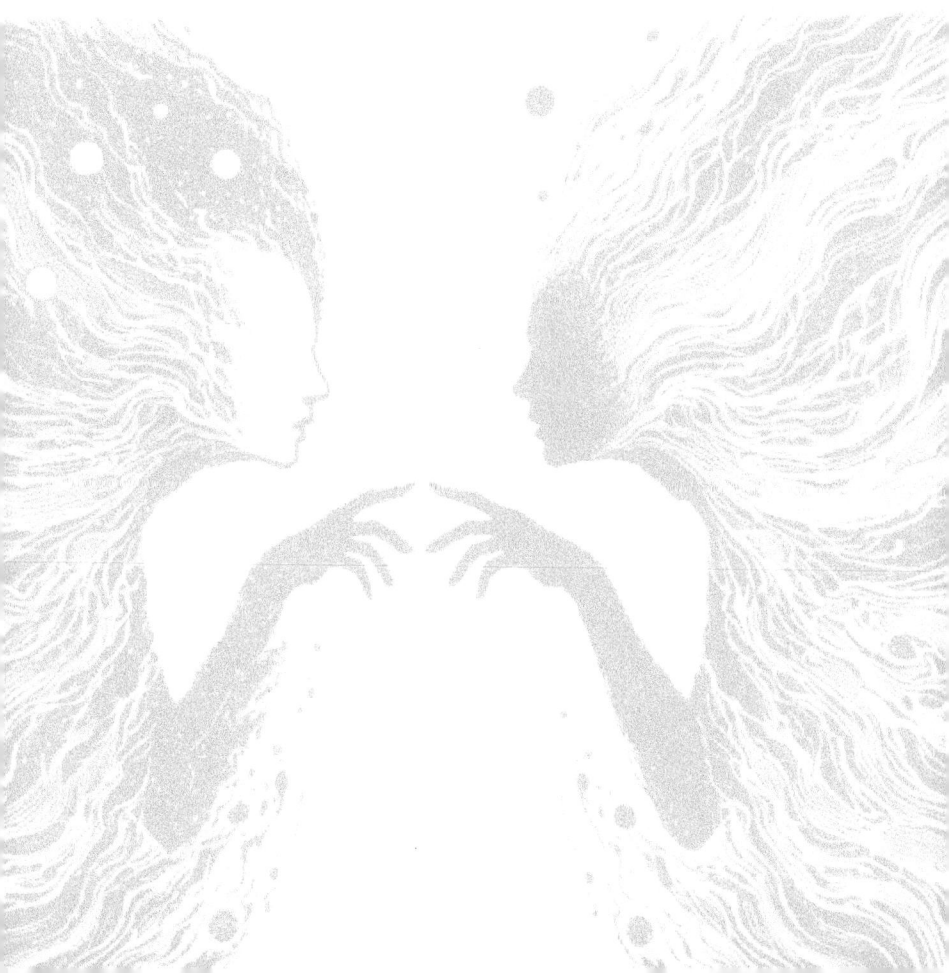

There is power in speaking the words we were told to keep buried.

Silence was never meant to be a prison.
It was never meant to suffocate truth.

This journey is about reclaiming voice,
unraveling shame,
and stepping into the light.

Because your story deserves to be heard.

No More Apologies

For so long, I swallowed my grief—
softened my words,
folded them into something
small enough to be ignored.

I learned to smile through the ache,
to sit with the weight of silence,
believing my pain would disappear
if I let it go unspoken.

But no more.

I will not shrink myself
to fit the comfort of others.
I will not apologize for existing
in my fullness.

This is my story—
my grief, my truth, my voice.
And it will be heard.

She Speaks

She carries a story
that once lived in whispers.
Taught to hold it in
like a shameful secret,
like it was hers alone to carry.

They told her
grief makes others uncomfortable.
They told her
some things are better left unsaid.
But silence never healed her.

So now,
she speaks.

Not for permission.
Not for applause.
But because her truth
doesn't belong in the shadows.

It is not a secret.
It is not a sin.

It is survival.
And it has a voice now.

Just for a Moment

It was only a flicker.
A soft sting
in the middle of your joy.

You were glowing—
telling me how it happened,
how you just knew.
And I smiled.

Really, I did.

But somewhere inside,
a small ache stirred.
Not anger.
Not envy.
Just the reminder
of what I'm still waiting for.

It passed—
like a breeze through curtains.
But for a moment,
I wanted
what came so easily
to you.

The Blame We Bear

They never ask him why we have no children.

They do not whisper behind his back.
They do not call him incomplete.

But me?

They measure me
by what I have not done.

By the children I have not borne.

It is my body they question.
It is my choices they judge.

But I refuse to carry their blame.
I refuse to let them make me less.

I am whole,
with or without a child to prove it.

The Fear of Saying It Aloud

There is fear
in the words I have yet to speak—
a tremor in my chest
every time I try to name
the grief that still sits heavy.

I wonder:
Will they understand?
Will they listen, or will they turn away?
Will my pain feel too much,
too raw,
too real?

But I cannot stay silent forever.
I cannot keep hiding in the quiet,
afraid of what my truth might cost.

So I speak,
and though my voice trembles,
it is mine.

For the Women Who Have Been Told to Stay Quiet

This is for you—
the ones who swallowed stories
so the room wouldn't grow uncomfortable.

For the women
who were told
grief should be private,
that pain makes you bitter,
that silence is strength.

You were never too much.
They were just afraid
of your truth.

Your story echoes
through the poems of strangers,
in the eyes of women
you've never met—
who carry the same ache
and the same hush.

You are not alone.
You never were.

Where I Come From

Where I come from,
babies come early—
expected like the seasons,
counted before they arrive.

At every family gathering,
there's a child on each hip,
a new pregnancy to announce,
and the quiet comparison
of timelines.

The women don't ask with malice—
but the words still land heavy:
"You're next, right?"
"Still nothing?"
"You better hurry."

I smile,
the way I was taught to.
But inside,
something shrinks.

Because where I come from,
motherhood is the standard,
the story already written for you.

And when you don't follow the script,
you become the silence in the room—
the one they don't quite know
how to speak to.

Still,
I keep showing up—
with love in my chest
and a different kind of bloom
in my hands.

JOURNEY FIVE

Redefining Self,
Redefining Motherhood

They told me motherhood was the only way to be whole.

But I have learned that creation takes many forms.

To love, to build, to heal, to give—
these are also ways of mothering.

This journey is for the ones who have had to redefine themselves,
for the ones who have had to unlearn the lies about what makes a woman complete.

This is where we claim a new story.
This is where we find freedom.

A New Definition

They asked me if I felt incomplete.
If I felt like I was missing something.

But I am not missing.

I am here, full and real and whole.

Motherhood is not the only way to create life.

I create love, art, laughter, warmth.
I have built a home inside myself.

I am not lacking.
I am enough.

This Body is Still Sacred

They told me my body was built for one thing.

That if it could not give life,
it was a failure.

But this body has held me through every storm.

This body has carried me up mountains.
This body has felt the sun on its skin and the wind in
its hair.

This body is not broken.

It is not unfinished work.

It is a temple, a home, a force.

This body is sacred.

The Quiet Between Us

I sit in circles that no longer fit,
smiling as they swap birth stories,
laughing in the right places,
hiding the hollow in my chest.

Their joy is not my enemy,
but some days, it feels like a door
that has locked me out.

They do not ask where I have been.
They do not see the ache
of being the one who never arrives.

I tuck my grief beneath the table,
next to untouched invitations
for baby showers I cannot bear to attend.

But I am learning—
that my path is not lesser, just different.
That I, too, am growing something beautiful.
That love, joy, and meaning
are not confined to one kind of story.

And when I sit at my own table,
I will set a place for myself—
whole, seen, enough.

Imagined Eyes

I've seen them—
your eyes in a smaller face,
my curls on a head
I've never held.

A child shaped by both of us—
not imagined,
but deeply known.

And when I speak of this longing,
the suggestions come quick:
"You can always adopt."
"What about a surrogate?"
"There are so many options."

As if love is enough
to sign papers,
cover costs,
or quiet the ache
for your own reflection
looking back at you.

I've looked into those paths—
walked the edges of them,
read the fine print,
felt the price
rise higher
than hope.

It's not that I wouldn't love another's child.
It's that I already love
the one I've never met—
the one with your smile
and my fire,
waiting in the space
between what is
and what will never be.

Roots and Legacy

I come from
women who knew how to hold pain
and still plant gardens.

From stories whispered
across oceans and altars.
From hands that stitched grief
into quilts of survival.

My roots are not broken—
they've just learned
to grow in silence.

I carry their strength,
even when I forget
where I come from.

The Village That Was

Once, mothers were forests—
their roots tangled in shared labor,
their branches sheltering each other's young.

Now, we are lone trees,
planted too far apart to whisper secrets
or share the weight of storms.

I dream of the village that was—
where no child was motherless,
and no mother was alone.

The Life I Have Created

They never told me
that life beyond loss could still be beautiful.
That motherhood doesn't need a name to be real.

They told me I would feel empty,
but I have learned to fill that space
with laughter, with love,
with all the ways I have learned to give.

I measure my life not in the moments I didn't get,
but in the ones I've found
on paths I never expected to walk.

I am creating something,
something rich and full.
A life that is mine—
and it is enough.

In the Quiet Rebuilding

I thought motherhood would look like one thing,
but it has shown up as something else.

It's not the vision I had.
It's not the future I once imagined.
And yet, there is something in me
that refuses to let it be only a loss.

I've learned to rebuild—
not from the ground up,
but from the pieces that remain.

I've found ways to nurture,
to create meaning,
even if it's not in the ways I thought it would be.

This is my path,
quiet and unassuming,
but full of purpose.

Not the motherhood I dreamed of,
but one that is mine,
still valid, still important.
Still whole.

Letting Go is Not Giving Up

I am not surrendering.
I am simply loosening my grip
on the life I thought I had to live
to make space for the one that is mine.

JOURNEY SIX

Healing & Enoughness

Healing is not a destination.
It is a language we learn to speak
after years of silence.

It is the way we move forward,
even with the weight of what we've lost.

This journey is for the ones
who are learning how to love themselves again.
For the ones who are learning
that they were never incomplete.

You are enough.
You have always been enough.

The First Time I Felt Light Again

It wasn't a grand moment—
no thunder breaking sky,
no revelation dressed in gold.

Just a morning
where the air moved softer,
like moss underfoot,
where breath returned
without asking if it belonged.

I stood at the edge of the ocean,
watching the waves
forget where they'd been,
and I realized—
I didn't have to carry it all.

Healing didn't arrive like a sunrise.
It crept in like tidewater—
slow, salt-laced, patient.

But that morning,
I let some of the weight return to the sea.

The Weight I Still Carry

Healing did not mean
I let go of you.
It meant I stopped trying
to outrun the ache.

It meant I learned
to speak your name softly,
like wind through pine,
without my voice breaking.

You are still here—
woven into me
like roots I cannot see,
but feel
every time the earth shifts.

I no longer carry you
as a wound.
Now, you are a whisper—
tender,
steady,
still mine.

The Life I Would've Given You

You would have known the ocean
before you knew a name.
Sunrises would've been your lullabies,
and pine needles your confetti.

We would have walked barefoot through gardens,
hands stained with dirt and peace,
teaching you how to listen—
to trees, to birds,
to the silence between.

You would've grown up
learning that stillness is not laziness,
that soft can be strong,
that joy lives in the small things.

We wouldn't have taught you to rush.
We would've taught you to return.
To breathe when the world moves too fast.
To feel. To feel everything.

I can't help but ache
for the child who never came,
and the life we would've shared—
not just full,
but sacred.

What No One Tells You About Healing

Healing is not a sunrise.
It doesn't arrive all at once,
flooding the dark with light.

Some mornings are easy—
a quiet breath,
a warm cup between your palms,
a stillness that feels almost like peace.

Other days, the ache returns
before your feet touch the floor.
Grief lingers in the steam of your coffee,
in the way the wind brushes your skin
like something once familiar.

No one tells you
how much starting over it takes.
How many days you'll spend relearning
how to live with the weight.

Healing is not about being strong.
It's not about forgetting.
It's learning to stay—
with the grief,
with the love,
with the parts of you still stitching themselves
whole.

It's not a single path.
It's every step you take
toward yourself.

Tired of Being Strong

I'm tired
of being called strong
like it's a compliment.

Tired of holding it together
while my insides unravel.

Tired of smiling
so no one gets uncomfortable,
of choosing grace
when what I really want
is to scream.

I don't want to be brave today.
I want to be held.
I want to break
without being told
how beautifully I'm breaking.

Enough

I spent years
trying to shape myself
into something more—
more gentle,
more certain,
less loud,
less needing.

I bent like a branch
in every direction,
hoping the world
would finally call me whole.

But now,
I stand rooted.
Not taller,
just truer.

I have nothing to prove.
No one to become.

I have always been enough—
wild, tender, whole.
Just like this.

Signs That I Am Becoming Whole

I know I am healing
because the sound of laughter
feels like home again.

Because I no longer flinch
at the sight of what I once prayed for.

Because my heart no longer feels
like it is walking through glass.

Because I am living,
not just waiting
for life to begin.

The Right to Keep Hoping

They say it's time
to let go.

But I still light candles
for dreams that haven't arrived,
still speak to the moon
like she's listening.

I carry questions
like prayer beads—
quiet, persistent, mine.

Hope still lives here.
Not loud,
but steady.

This is not denial.
This is devotion.

The Silence of God

They told me faith would carry me through,
but they never told me what to do
when my prayers fell into silence.

When I held my hands together,
but nothing held me back.

When I searched for signs,
but found only quiet where faith used to be.

They told me God never leaves,
but grief made the world so quiet
that I wondered if He had.

And yet,
in the middle of my sorrow,
I still whispered His name.

Not because I was certain,
but because hope is sometimes the only thing
stronger than doubt.

What the Wind Will Remember

They said
you'd have nothing to show
for your years.
As if memory
only lives in names.

But the wind
will remember your voice
on those mornings
you walked barefoot
into the garden
just to say thank you.

The ocean will remember
the way you stood
against waves
without flinching.

Trees will speak your name
in root language.
You have touched
the pulse of things
unseen.

What you've planted
won't look like them—
but it will grow.

The Version of Me That Never Gave Up

She lived through seasons
that never bloomed.

She cried in locked bathrooms,
holding her own body
like it was the only thing left
that hadn't walked away.

She counted months
like prayers on a rosary,
burned sage,
swallowed needles,
lit candles with shaking hands—
and still rose,
barefoot,
into mornings that offered nothing new.

No one saw her.
But I did.

I remember the way
she held grief in her ribs
and still found space to breathe.
I remember how she looked in the mirror,
and stayed.

She is every version of me
that refused to disappear.

I build my life
on the ground she refused to surrender.

She is the roots,
and I—
I am the bloom.

A Quiet Promise

In the stillness of the night,
when the ache feels too vast,
know this—
you are not forgotten.

Not by the earth beneath your feet,
not by the stars that quietly watch over you.

Grief is a language,
and so is hope.

Though the world may not see your heartache,
there is space within you
where your light still lingers—
waiting, gently, to bloom.

You are more than this silence,
more than the labels they've placed on you.

You are a promise in the making.

And in time,
the weight will soften,
as the body learns
to carry both the grief and the growth.

JOURNEY SEVEN

Light After the Storm

There was a time I thought
I would never feel light again.

But here I am,
breathing deeply, loving fully, standing taller.

This journey is a celebration.
Of survival.
Of rediscovering joy.
Of knowing that the storm does not last forever.

You are here.
And you are still becoming.

Healing is not just about what you leave behind.
It is about what you step into.

To the One Who Is Still Healing

If you are still healing—
moving slowly,
breathing through the ache—
know this:

You are not late.
You are not broken.

You are growing
in places the world cannot see.

Some days will open like petals,
easy, tender, full of light.
Others will close like fists,
and that, too, is part of it.

Even in the silence,
you are becoming.

You do not have to bloom all at once.
You are allowed to take your time.

You are already enough.

The First Time I Laughed Without Guilt

It happened in a way so small,
I almost missed it—
a laugh, unguarded,
spilling out of me like sunlight
through an open window.

For so long, I carried sorrow
like an oath,
as if joy was a betrayal,
as if healing meant forgetting.

But the wind did not ask permission
to dance against my skin.
The waves did not check
if I was ready to rise with them.

Life had been waiting for me—
not to move on,
but to move with it.

And so, I laughed.
Not because I was healed,
but because, for the first time,
I was allowed to be both—
a woman who remembers
and a woman who still reaches for joy.

A Love Letter to My Body

Dear Body,

I am sorry for the way I have spoken to you.

For the way I have blamed you, doubted you,
called you names that were never yours to carry.

You have held me through everything.
Through grief, through fear, through healing.

You have never stopped trying, never stopped
breathing,
never stopped carrying me forward.

I see you now.
I honor you now.
And I will love you better.

With gratitude,
Mind & Soul

I Am Not Who I Was

I used to think healing meant
going back to who I used to be.

But I am not her anymore.

I am softer, but stronger.
I carry scars, but also wisdom.

I have known loss, but I have also known love.

I do not want to go back.

I am too busy becoming
someone even more powerful than before.

The Light That Finds Us

Healing isn't a sudden burst.
It doesn't blaze in like sunrise—
it unfolds like soft light through leaves,
quiet, patient, almost shy.

It's not the light I imagined—
bright and instant.
It's the glow that comes slowly,
like morning warmth on bare skin
or the hush of wind moving through trees.

The things that heal me
are small and steady—
a laugh that catches me off guard,
the way my breath evens in silence,
how the sun touches my shoulders
without asking if I'm ready.

Light doesn't knock.
It doesn't wait for permission.
It just returns—
in its own way,
in its own time,
finding its way back into the cracks
that grief once sealed.

The Life That Still Awaits Me

There are paths
still calling my name—
sunsets I have not stood beneath,
rivers I have yet to follow.

There are stories
still tucked inside my chest,
waiting for the right silence
to open.

Life is not just
what I lost.

It is the hush before dawn.
The unopened bloom.
The yes I haven't spoken yet.

And I am walking toward it—
not with certainty,
but with open hands.

Exactly Here

I stopped asking,
"What comes next?"

I looked around
and realized
I had already arrived.

This joy?
This stillness?

It's not the backup plan.
It's the life I built—
and it is beautiful.

And Yet, I Rise

I have stood in waiting rooms filled with quiet
prayers,
sat in cars where silence was heavier than words.

I have swallowed grief in the dark,
let hope slip between my fingers more times than I
can count.

And yet—

I rise.

Not as the woman I was before.
Not as the woman I once prayed I would be.

But as the woman I am now—
softer, wiser, still standing.

Healing is not the absence of scars.
It is the choice to keep moving forward
even when the past still lingers.

And so, I take one more step.
And another.
And another.

Because even in the aftermath of what I lost—

I am still here.
I am still growing.
I am still becoming.

POETIC NECTAR COLLECTIVE
A Sanctuary of Words

I didn't know this book would become something more.

But somewhere between loss and language, it opened—
into a quiet place where grief felt safe,
and silence could speak.

In that stillness, expression took root.
Art became a way through.
Words became a way home.

And from that same soil,
Poetic Nectar Collective *began to grow.*

Poetic Nectar Collective: *A sacred space where the unspoken becomes creation.*

Some stories are too heavy to carry alone. Some grief, too vast for a single heart to hold. But when expression meets tenderness, something begins to shift—grief becomes something sacred, something seen.

Poetic Nectar Collective was born from that truth: that healing deepens when it's shared, that art can hold what words cannot, and that no one should have to carry invisible pain alone.

This space is more than poetry. It's a garden—a place where sorrow is planted with care, and creativity becomes a way to begin again. What grows here is soft, slow, and intentional: poetry, offerings, and reflections born from the ache of what was lost and the quiet hope of what might still bloom.

You are welcome here. With your grief. With your longing. With your becoming.

If you've ever felt like your pain had no place to land, let it land here. Let it be witnessed. Let it become something. To share your story, your art, or your voice, use the hashtag **#PoeticNectar** and find yourself among those who understand.

We are already waiting for you.

A Love Letter in Echoes

We are a garden of voices—each different, each essential. Some stories arrive like thunder. Others bloom in quiet, steady resilience.

Jessica's voice is one of those quiet blooms. Soft. Strong. Honest. Her words carry the weight of loss with grace and offer light to those who have walked through similar shadows.

Her poetry is not just personal—it's universal. It speaks to the women who have held life in their bodies, even for a moment, and to the ones who continue loving through absence.

Her story lives here now—as part of this garden, as part of the collective, as part of the many women who carry love in places no one else can see.

Her voice continues in the pages that follow—woven into this garden, just as it was always meant to be.

I Could Cry. I Do Cry.

From deep within my soul,
I grieve in silence,
when my heart feels lonely.

I mourn with no tears, no screams,
when I feel empty inside,
and a breath of pain overflows,
realizing I've lost a little life inside my womb.

Heartbreak In My Womb

When my womb held a second blessing,
hope briefly bloomed but was soon
overshadowed by fear and heartbreak.

In my sorrow,
I yearned for a comforting call from the doctor,
but every call brought less hope and more tears.

Time passed swiftly,
much like the tears streaming down my face.

Once again,
I found myself in the painful realization
of losing another life within my womb.

Blink of Happiness

We prayed to keep you,
but you slipped away,
for the third time.

Like a river overflowing,
gone in disarray.

Nights of prayers,
yet not enough.

Here we stand,
rebuilding hopes,
facing our fears.

Hoping,
praying,
dreaming,
you'll return to stay,
bring us joy again,
in a brighter day.

We are not meant to walk through grief alone.
We are not meant to rush through it, either.

What follows isn't a solution—it's simply an
offering.
A quiet place to begin again, in your own way, at
your own pace.

GUIDE TO HEALING
A Soft Offering

Healing is not a checklist.
Not a linear path.
It is a tide, pulling you forward
then back again—
a rhythm, an unfolding.

There is no "right" way to heal.
Only movement.
Only breath.
Only finding yourself, again and again,
in the spaces where light seeps through.

So here, I offer you not instructions,
but small rituals—
whispers of what has helped me
when the weight was too much.

Take what you need.
Leave what does not call to you.

Let healing be a slow return to yourself.

Healing Through Nature: *A Return to Belonging*

Walk barefoot on the earth.
Let it remind you:
you are rooted,
even when you feel untethered.

Sit by the water,
whisper your grief to the waves,
watch them carry it away
without asking for it back.

Healing Through Breath & Sound: *The Body's Quiet Rebellion*

Inhale deeply—four counts in.
Hold—four counts still.
Exhale slowly—six counts out.
Repeat until your body softens,
until you remember: you are alive.

Sing, hum, let your voice vibrate through you.
Your sound is proof
that you have never been silent.

Listen to music that stirs your soul.
Let it pull you into memory, into presence, into feeling.

Healing Through Ritual: *Marking the Invisible*

Light a candle for yourself.
Sit with it.
Watch the flame and whisper
the words you longed to hear.
Let them no longer be missing.

Hold a stone in your hands.
Press your grief into it.
Then release it back to the earth—
it will carry what you no longer need.

Write a letter to the parts of yourself
that still ache.
Then burn it,
bury it,
or let the wind take it.
Some things are meant to be released.

Healing Through Art: *Letting the Pain Speak*

Paint your grief—
not for beauty,
not for others,
but because your pain
deserves to exist outside of your body.

Write poetry,
even if no one will ever read it.
Even if the only one who understands it
is you.

Move, dance, let your body tell the story
that words cannot hold.

Healing Through Stillness: *The Art of Being*

Sit beneath the night sky.
Let the vastness remind you—
your sorrow is not all there is.

Hold a warm cup of tea in your hands.
Feel the heat, the grounding,
the presence of this single moment.

Healing is not only in movement.
It is also in staying.

FINAL REFLECTION

Grief doesn't end.
But it softens.
It changes shape.
And in the quiet that follows, something else begins to bloom.

Maybe it's the quiet decision to begin again.
Maybe it's a walk through the trees.
Maybe it's just the permission to feel without fixing.

This book is not a conclusion.
It's a companion. A mirror.
A breath to return to when the weight is too much or the world moves too fast.

And if you've made it here—thank you.
For staying. For feeling. For reading these pages with your whole self.

You were never alone.
You're still not.
And you never have to be.

You made it to the garden.
Stay as long as you need.

Appendix: *Where to Find Light*

Resources & Support for Healing

Healing is not something we do in isolation.
It is something we do in connection, community, and love.
Below are resources to help you find support, strength, and
light on your journey.

Global Support & Advocacy Organizations

North America

RESOLVE: The National Infertility Association – Advocacy, support groups, and resources for individuals experiencing infertility. https://resolve.org/

The Broken Brown Egg – Support and awareness for Black women experiencing infertility.
https://thebrokenbrownegg.org/

Still Mothers – Support for women facing life without children after infertility or loss. https://stillmothers.com/

Europe

Fertility Network UK – Counseling, grants, and support groups across the UK. https://fertilitynetworkuk.org/

Childless Not By Choice (UK & Global) – Online support for women navigating involuntary childlessness.
https://cnbc.org.uk/

Women's Health Concern (UK) – Resources on fertility, miscarriage, and reproductive health.
https://womens-health-concern.org/

Asia & Africa

Bumba Foundation (Nigeria) – Fertility care access, education, and stigma-breaking initiatives.
https://bumbafoundation.org/

Mothers in Waiting (South Africa) – Infertility support for African women, breaking cultural silence.
https://mothersinwaiting.org.za/

Pink Orchid Foundation (India) – Fertility education and emotional support in India. https://pinkorchidfoundation.org/

Australia & New Zealand

SANDS Australia – 24/7 pregnancy loss helpline, memorial events, and advocacy for bereaved parents.
https://sands.org.au/

Fertility New Zealand – Support networks and fertility information across New Zealand. https://fertilitynz.org.nz/

The Pink Elephants Support Network (Australia) –
Miscarriage and early pregnancy loss support.
https://pinkelephants.org.au/

Latin America & Caribbean

Red Nacional Infértiles (Spain & Latin America) – Support for Spanish-speaking individuals facing infertility. https://redinfertiles.com/

Grupo de Apoyo Infertilidad Argentina (GAIA) – Resources and legal support for women experiencing infertility in Argentina. https://infertilidadargentina.org/

Online Communities & Digital Support

Poetic Nectar Collective (Social Media Movement)
Use the hashtag #PoeticNectar to share your poetry, art, and story.

Gateway Women (Worldwide) – A global network for women facing involuntary childlessness. https://gateway-women.com/

Silent Sorority (Global Forum) – An online community redefining life after infertility. https://silentsorority.com/

Reddit Support Groups:

r/infertility – Peer support for those navigating treatments & loss. https://www.reddit.com/r/infertility/

r/childfreeafterinfertility – For those moving forward without children. https://www.reddit.com/r/childfreeafterinfertility/

Crisis & Mental Health Support

Postpartum Support International (Global) – Support for miscarriage & infertility-related depression.
https://www.postpartum.net/

Samaritans (UK & Global) – 24/7 mental health helpline.
https://www.samaritans.org/

Crisis Text Line (US, UK, Canada, Australia) – For emotional support during infertility struggles.
https://www.crisistextline.org/

Discussion Questions & Reflection

Healing is a journey, and every reader will take something different from these pages.

These questions are meant to guide you in deeper reflection, whether you are reading alone or discussing with others.

For Personal Reflection or Book Clubs:

- **Which poem resonated with you the most? Why?**

- **What is one way you have found healing in your own life?**

- **How has grief shaped your understanding of love and resilience?**

- **What would you say to your past self—the one who was struggling the most?**

- **What emotions did this book bring up for you? How did they sit with you?**

- **What does it mean to 'redefine motherhood' in your own life?**

- **How do you practice self-compassion, and what does healing look like to you?**

- **What is one thing you are grateful for in this moment?**

Acknowledgments

This book wasn't written alone—even if much of it began in silence.

To the women who trusted me with their truths, who reminded me that we're never as alone as we feel— thank you.

To Jessica, for lending your voice and your ache to this garden. Your presence here is sacred.

To my husband—for holding space for my wholeness, again and again.

To every friend, sister, healer, and artist who met me with tenderness instead of answers— this book carries a piece of you, too.

And to the part of me that kept writing through it all— thank you for staying.

www.ingramcontent.com/pod-product-compliance
Lightning Source LLC
Chambersburg PA
CBHW051631120626
46551CB00014B/2029